3/05

WI

EARTH'S CHANGING LANDSCAPE

Population Growth

Philip Steele

First published in 2003 by Franklin Watts
Franklin Watts, 96 Leonard Street, London EC2A 4XD

Franklin Watts Australia
45–51 Huntley Street, Alexandria, NSW 2015
This edition published under license from Franklin Watts. All rights reserved.

Series Editor: Sarah Peutrill; Series Designer: Simon Borrough; Art Director: Jonathan Hair; Picture Researcher: Juliet Duff; Series Consultant: Steve Watts, FRGS, Principal Lecturer in Geography Education at the University of Sunderland

Published in the United States by Smart Apple Media
1980 Lookout Drive, North Mankato, Minnesota 56003

Library of Congress Control Number: 2004102619

ISBN 1-58340-480-5

9 8 7 6 5 4 3 2 1

Picture Credits:
Adina Tovy Amsel/Eye Ubiquitous: 25. Sebastian Bolesch/Still Pictures: 35t. Jon Bower/Ecoscene: 11. Andrew Brown/Ecoscene: 17. Howard Brundrett/Eye Ubiquitous: 28. D. Cummings/Eye Ubiquitous: 33. Daniel Dancer/Still Pictures: 7t. Nigel Dickinson/Still Pictures: 14b. Digital Vision: 14t, 18, 20, 26, 29, 30, 31, 32. Mark Edwards/Still Pictures: 13. K.Glaser/Custom Medical Stock/SPL: 42. Sylvia Greenland/Eye Ubiquitous: 24. L. Hong/UNEP/Still Pictures: 16. Earl & Nazima Kowall/Corbis: 34. Frank Leather/Eye Ubiquitous: 22. Sally Morgan/Ecoscene: 38. Knut Mueller/Still Pictures: 39t. NASA/SPL: 43. Christine Osborne/Ecoscene: 15, 39b. Edward Parker/Still Pictures: front cover, endpapers, 6. Geoff Redmayne/Eye Ubiquitous: 9. Leon Scadeberg/Eye Ubiquitous: 27. Jorgen Schytte/Still Pictures: 21. Sipa/Rex Features: 37. Charlie Pye-Smith/Still Pictures: 7b, 40. Mike Southern/Eye Ubiquitous: 8. Sean Sprague/Still Pictures: 35b, 41. Jochen Tack/Still Pictures: 23. Paul Thompson/Eye Ubiquitous: 10. David Turnley/Corbis: 36. Voltchev-UNEP/Still Pictures: 19.

CONTENTS

THE HUMAN LANDSCAPE

Tens of thousands of years ago, a hunter could track animals for months and never see another human in the empty landscape. Today, it is hard to find a spot to be alone for five minutes. Our world is now home to about 6.2 billion people, and that number is growing.

Living on Earth As humans, we are part of the natural world. The **environment** has made us the way we are. It has affected the way we look and the way we behave. We have changed the natural world as well, by taking the water, food, and resources from it that we need in order to stay alive.

People and nature All living creatures must adapt to the natural environment in this way. They use the planet and are shaped by the planet. As humans, however, we can go one stage further. By using our intelligence, we can change the environment to suit our needs. That is the secret of our success as a species. However, this ability does hold downsides, both for us and for the planet on which we live.

Digging and delving Humans have always had an instinct to dig and delve. Stone Age people learned to dig out flints and to flake them until they had razor-sharp edges. They made axes with them to cut down forests. They changed the world in which they lived.

Brazil has a **population** of 176.5 million, and eight out of every 10 people live in towns or cities. Its natural rate of increase is currently 1.3 percent each year.

This landscape in Washington state has been stripped bare by loggers. No cover remains for wildlife, and the soil is exposed to wind, rain, and ice.

Building roads around the Channel rail tunnel in southern England destroyed the natural environment of the Farthingloe valley.

Changing the landscape As the human population of the world grew, its effect on the natural world increased. Today, great cities stretch across the plains. Railroads and highways cut through hills and across rivers. Most of the visible countryside is divided into cultivated fields. There are still huge areas of wilderness, but in the future, these may also be touched by human activities.

POPULATING THE PLANET

As humans evolved or developed, they interacted with their environment. This interaction caused their numbers to rise or fall. The numbers of humans never dropped for very long. Over the ages, the world's population rose steadily. People spread around the globe.

A small world In about 15,000 B.C., the world's population was only five million. People lived by hunting herds of large animals and gathering plants. They could not ensure a reliable source of food and had to wander as the herds migrated season by season.

Farms and cities By 5,000 B.C., the world's population had reached about 66 million. The climate was warming, making it possible for more people to learn how to farm. They could settle in one place and plant crops. This made starvation less common. Life was safer inside the walled towns and cities that were being built.

Bronze and iron The mining and working of metals led to the stripping of woodland by axes, to better plows, but also to deadlier weapons. The world's population continued to increase, reaching 250 million around 2,000 years ago. Ships and boats were helping people settle and farm new lands.

These fields in Peru were dug by Inca farmers 500 years ago.

Plague and war During the Middle Ages (around A.D. 500–1475), there were terrible diseases. By A.D. 1000, the world population had dipped to about 240 million. After this, it grew once again, despite major setbacks caused by repeated outbreaks of deadly infectious diseases such as bubonic plague, which killed millions. Farming, trade, and settlement all suffered. Because there were fewer people, those workers who did survive could bargain for more money for the work they did.

Follow it through: farming and population

People lived by hunting and following herds of wild animals

People learned to plant seeds, which offered them food in the same place the following year

Take it further

Pay a visit to an old cemetery and look at the graves.

◆ Did people die younger in the 1800s or the 1900s?
◆ What might explain the difference?
◆ Do any gravestones say how people died?
◆ Do any gravestones say what people did for a living?
◆ Look at the information you have found out. How might it have affected your local community or the countryside?

This is the winding gear that lowered miners to the coalface during the industrial age of the 1800s and 1900s.

Rapid growth In the 1500s and 1600s, the world's population raced ahead once more, reaching about 679 million by 1700. This was a great new age of **global** exploration and trade. People tended to have large families. One reason was that without machinery, many hands were still needed to run a farm. Another reason people had large families was to make up for the fact that many children died in their infancy or as young adults.

A new age The 1800s saw a new age of science, medicine, and healthcare, and of technology, transportation, and industry. As a result, the world's population reached about 1.63 billion by 1900. The landscape was mined, farmed, and built over as never before.

People stayed in the same place year after year, building a town

Any extra food farmers grew could be traded for other goods

The land was soon covered in fields, buildings, and roads

HUMANS EVERYWHERE

After the 1900s, the population of the world grew very quickly. By 1920, there were 1.96 billion people. By 1950, there were 2.52 billion, and by 1990, 5.29 billion. Today, the 6 billion mark is already behind us. This has been described as a **population explosion.**

High-rise Hong Kong, home to 6.8 million people.

A crowded world Many parts of the world, such as hot deserts or icy wastelands, are not suitable for human settlement. Most people live where there is food, water, and a chance to work. In the last 100 years, some of these regions have become very crowded. In Bangladesh, the **population density** has increased to 2,405 people per square mile (928 per sq km). In smaller built-up areas, such as the Chinese region of Macao, there are 57,369 people per square mile (22,150 per sq km).

Follow it through: medical advances  Large numbers of people die from a disease ➤ Scientists learn how to prevent or cure the disease ➤ Fewer people die and the population rises

Industry creates work and wages, shops, streets, and traffic. About five million people live in the Chinese city of Shenyang.

Why so many? The main reason that the population explosion took place was better healthcare. People could prevent diseases with **immunization**. People learned why diseases happened and how to save lives with new medicines, such as antibiotics. Many more mothers and infants survived childbirth.

Another reason for the population rise was improvement in the water supply, crop yields, food quality, and diet. All of these factors helped people to live longer and live better.

What about the planet? The existence of so many people in the world has a huge effect on the environment. People need food, water, and shelter just to exist. They create waste. They use fuel; they build dams. The more people there are, the more the world is changed.

Case study: China

The fertility of the plains, river banks, and coasts of eastern China has made this region one of the most populated places on Earth for thousands of years. The chief risks to the population have always been extreme earthquakes and floods. However, population growth was supported at an early date by **intensive farming** and new technology, by organized government and protection within walled cities.

Population explosion

The global population explosion of the last 50 years has been at its most extreme in China. Today, its population is the world's highest, at 1,288,700,000 —20 percent of everyone living on Earth, in an area that covers only seven percent of the total area of the globe occupied by people. Cities such as Chonqing are expanding very quickly as many poor farm workers leave the land to seek jobs in towns. As the population grows, settlers are also moving into inhospitable mountains, forests, and deserts in the western half of the country. The newcomers are clearing forest, irrigating dry regions for farming, and building new roads.

More people give birth, and the population soars ➤ The land cannot provide enough food, living space, or employment ➤ More land must be used for farming or building, or people must move elsewhere

NUMBERS AND PLANNING

To find out how many people live in the world, they need to be officially counted. This is called taking a **census**. The results then have to be studied to see whether the population is rising or falling, and the results help planners decide how resources should be used. The study of population is called **demography**.

Growth rates The rate at which the world population is growing each year is about 1.3 percent. This may seem high, but the growth rate has actually been falling over the last 30 years. That does not mean that the number of births is falling, but it does tell us that the population explosion is beginning to level off.

World population figures tell a story that is determined by many factors, including climate, resources, economics, transportation, healthcare, and cultural values.

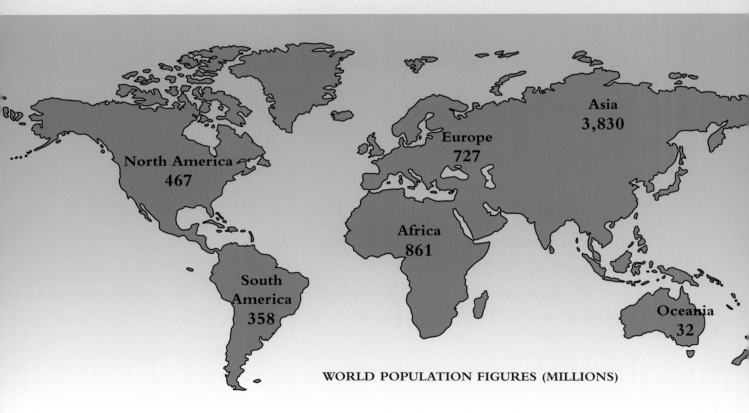

Asia
3,830

Europe
727

North America
467

Africa
861

South America
358

Oceania
32

WORLD POPULATION FIGURES (MILLIONS)

Follow it through: school size

The government takes a census

The number of children in each area is calculated

Future plans

Demography is useful because it helps people plan for the future and measure the impact of humans on the environment. As scientists monitor the loss of forests, the pollution of the sea, or the spread of cities, our knowledge of population growth and density helps us to find explanations and seek solutions.

How many children?

The population growth rate is at its highest in Africa (2.4 percent each year). Because many African countries are poor, people want to have a large number of children to bring in as much income as possible. They also fear losing children to hunger or illness. Having large families has become a tradition. This used to be the case in Europe, too, but no longer. In Europe, the growth rate is the world's lowest, currently falling by 0.1 percent per year. Because it is a wealthier continent, smaller families have more economic power and a better chance of survival.

Fewer babies

In the last 100 years, governments and international organizations have tried to reduce the rate at which the population is growing. Many have introduced policies of **birth control**. They encourage couples to use **contraception** so that they have fewer babies. Some religious groups oppose contraception because they are against the prevention of life. Some countries have tried to limit the size of families, either by law or by rewarding people for having small families. China brought in a one-child-per-family policy. Many people criticized this because it took away people's personal right to choose.

Take it further

Find out about your own family history.

- Ask each of your grandparents how many brothers or sisters they had.
- If you can, find out about your great-grandparents as well.
- How many brothers or sisters do you and your parents have?
- Make a family tree. Which generation had the highest birth rate? Which had the lowest?

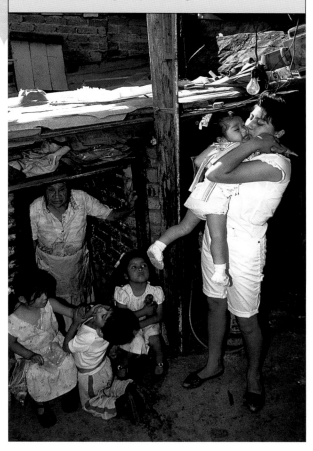

A population explosion in Mexico City has resulted in crowded, poor quality housing.

| Educational needs for each area are monitored | In some areas, more classroom space is needed | More schools are built |
| | In some areas, less space is needed | Schools are closed, and buildings are redeveloped for other uses |

PEOPLE AND ANIMALS

As humans, we share the environment with animals and plants. All living things interact with each other within local environments, or **ecosystems**. The way we treat animals has a major effect on Earth's changing landscape.

In the wild Wild animals help to create and shape landscapes. They may graze on certain plants or help to spread seeds. They may dig the soil or fertilize it with their droppings. When the animals disappear, the landscape changes. As populations grow, towns and roads spread into the landscape. This destroys the habitat of wild animals. Many large African mammals can now survive only within fenced-off reserves.

Thousands of elephants, shapers of the African savannah, are killed illegally. Their tusks are traded for their ivory.

Australian sheep stations (large sheep farms) can be the size of a small nation.

Hunting Humans have always eaten wild animals and fish. If too many are hunted and killed, an entire species may become scarce or **extinct**. But hunting cannot support a large human population. In today's crowded world, only a very small number of people still live by hunting.

New pastures Humans invented farming because it is a more efficient way of producing food than hunting. **Domesticated** animals supply us with meat, milk, hides or wool, and horn. To do this, they need good pasture. Meadow land or pasture now occupies about 20 percent of the world's land surface.

Follow it through: overgrazing

Herders move into thin, dry grassland

Their goats destroy trees and shrubs

Overgrazing

As populations rise, herders are forced onto thinner grassland. If there is too much grazing, this can quickly turn to desert. This is happening in Africa's Sahel region, to the south of the Sahara Desert. Overgrazing accounts for about 35 percent of soil degradation worldwide.

Large herds of goats soon strip the soil bare in Morocco, a land of mountains and deserts.

Land use

Ranching—cattle farming—is now a big international industry. But some people think it is not the best way to feed a hungry world. Two and a half acres (1 ha) planted with soybeans can produce 22 times as much protein as the same amount of land used as pasture for cattle. With the world population growing, the way we use land may have to change so that every part is used in the most effective way.

Case study: Ranching in Brazil

Since the 1960s, large areas of the Amazon River basin in Brazil have been used for cattle ranching. A market for cheap beef in North America encouraged this process. The profits were quick and short-lived, while the damage to the environment has been extreme and long-lasting. Much of the grazing area has been cleared of tropical rainforest by burning. Such soil is not natural pasture and soon degrades. Full tropical forest, which includes slow-growing hardwood trees, has no time to recover before the soil becomes eroded by wind or rain.

Vegetation dies, and no roots are left to trap moisture and bind the soil

In a drought, the soil can turn to dust and be blown away by the wind

FEEDING THE WORLD

Plants are the most important source of food for humans. We depend on basic, or staple, crops such as wheat, rice, and corn for our survival. Cultivation of these and other plants has altered natural landscapes all around the world.

Arable land Some of the world's first agriculture took place near rivers, where flood waters left behind fertile mud each year. People have since learned to grow crops in almost every kind of natural environment—on grasslands, in cleared woodland or forest, in wetlands, and on mountains. Arable land (used for cultivation) now takes up about 10 percent of Earth's surface.

Rice is the staple crop of China and is mostly grown in flooded paddy fields. In highland areas, terraced fields are cut from the slopes. Low walls allow irrigation and prevent soil erosion.

Case study: Farming in Bangladesh

Bangladesh is the most crowded country in the world. Most of its people farm the green, lush plains around the river Ganges and its delta. As the population has grown, plains dwellers have moved into more remote areas of the country, such as the Chittagong Hill Tract. There, the traditional way of farming (known as *jhum,* or "slash-and-burn") has always been to cut and burn a forest clearing, cultivate it for a period, and then move on, letting the forest grow back again. The rise in settlement means that there is no longer enough space left for this traditional farming method, so now land is being turned into permanent fields and banana **plantations**.

Take it further

Collect newspaper or magazine articles on the GM debate, or search the Internet.

◆ What are the main arguments for GM?
◆ What are the main arguments against GM?
◆ How might the use of GM crops affect the less economically developed countries of the world?

Genetically modified corn undergoes a trial planting in the state of Illinois. Some people are concerned about how GM crops will affect the environment.

Feeding the millions With the population explosion of the 1900s, humans had to find ways to use the same amount of land and still feed everyone. This led to intensive farming, which meant that the amount produced could be increased with no increase in costs. This was achieved by farming fewer types of crops on one farm, and by farming larger fields using artificial **fertilizers** and **pesticides**. Agriculture became a large-scale global industry. Today, countries should be able to produce enough food for everyone. Even so, one in every six people in the world still goes hungry as a result of drought, floods, war, poor distribution, unfair trading systems, or poor farming policies.

New crops? Another way to increase food yields is to introduce new super-crops, which, for example, are resistant to drought or produce more grain. One method of breeding crops is called **genetic modification** (GM). Scientists alter a plant's genes, which pass its characteristics down from one generation to the next. GM helps to give a plant particular qualities, such as resistance to weeds or pests. Scientists who support GM claim it could be of great benefit to the world's less developed countries. Other scientists disagree and fear it could have a harmful effect on natural ecosystems.

PRECIOUS WATER

The more people there are on Earth, the more water is needed. Over 70 percent of Earth's surface is covered in water. The trouble is that most of the water is salty, and humans need fresh water. They need to drink it every day to stay alive, and they need it for growing crops.

Drinking water   In more economically developed countries, water is removed from rivers and reservoirs and treated with chemicals and filtered before use. In less economically developed regions of the world, water may be taken directly from wells or rivers that are not clean.

More than a billion people worldwide lack safe drinking water. This is a major cause of disease. In 2003, delegates from 182 countries meeting at the World Water Forum in Kyoto, Japan, agreed to the goal of reducing the number of those without a safe and clean water supply by half before the year 2015.

In Ethiopia, women may have to walk long distances to the nearest well. Drought is common and only 25 percent of water supplies are clean and healthy.

Water shortages When water supplies become insufficient for the needs of a growing population, the first priority is to use less. All unnecessary use of water must be restricted by law. In northern China, where 110 cities face severe water shortages, people have been limited to 6.6 gallons (25 l) of water a day, and industrial output has had to be reduced.

To solve this problem, China has begun a project to divert the Huang He (Yellow River) to bring it through the most populous regions and conserve supply. It is the country's third-biggest water project, and it is expected to divert 157 million cubic yards (120 million cu m) of the river.

New sources of water are always the first priority, but this may cause conflict between thirsty cities, regions, or nations. If one location draws off water, another must do without. An increasing world population means that the resolution of such conflicts is essential for survival.

Take it further
Find out where the water in your own home comes from. Where is it treated?

◆ Measure how much water or other liquid you drink in one day. You can do this by using a measuring cup or reading the information on a can or carton.
◆ Can you determine how much you drink in a year?
◆ What other things do people in your home use water for?

Watering the fields
Around 69 percent of all the water we use is for farming. Water for irrigation can be carried to the crops by pipelines or open channels. Irrigation can have amazing effects, such as transforming a whole region and turning deserts green. But, with a growing population, there is a conflict between how much water is saved for people to drink and how it is used for producing food.

Irrigation in Libya makes it possible to cultivate the fringes of the desert.

TREES AND PEOPLE

About one-third of Earth's surface is covered in trees. Wooded regions take many forms around the world, from northern evergreen forests, to temperate woodlands and tropical rainforests. These are the richest natural **habitats** in the world.

Deforestation As the world's population rises, the forests are vanishing. Since the end of the last Ice Age around 10,000 B.C., half of the world's forests have been destroyed by humans. An area of forest larger than Greece is currently lost to the world each year.

Timber traders Loggers cut down trees to supply the furniture and building industries. Timber is pulped to make paper. Forests are cleared to make way for farms, plantations, mines, and towns. A lot of wood is also cleared by poor villagers to use as fuel.

A life force We need forests because they absorb the waste gas carbon dioxide and pump out life-giving oxygen in its place. They give out fresh water in the form of vapor. Their roots bind the soil together, so if they are cut down, the soil soon erodes. When burned down, the fumes add pollution to the atmosphere around Earth.

The rainforests of Sabah state, in northern Borneo, Malaysia, have been greatly depleted by logging. This timber will probably be exported to Japan.

What can be done? International agreements and laws already limit logging in many areas. However, illegal logging is hard to control because it often takes place in remote areas of poor countries.

More and more forests around the world are protected or managed so that they are sustainable. This means that the felling of trees is carefully controlled and that new trees are planted to replace them. Many companies selling, for example, garden furniture or decking now try to buy their wood from sustainable forests.

In Central America and Australia, some tropical forests now offer **eco-tourism**. There, visitors may study the rainforest ecology without destroying the forest. The money created helps to sustain traditional communities.

Follow it through: forests

Loggers build a road across a region of rainforest

Settlements are built alongside the road

A young girl carries a heavy bundle of firewood to market in Kathmandu, capital of Nepal. The fuel is used for cooking and heating.

Case study: Deforestation in Nepal

Nepal is a mountainous country in the Himalayas. Its population of 25.2 million is growing rapidly, due in part to improved healthcare. People need food, so large areas of forest in Nepal are being cut down to create terraced fields or pasture. Wood is also gathered in large quantities to heat houses. Deforestation has led to soil erosion, increased water run-off, and the swelling of countless mountain streams. This has increased flooding far downstream, where the streams flow into great rivers such as the Ganges.

The settlers kill wild animals and clear ground for farming	Areas of the forest are divided by roads and towns into small pockets	The natural environment is destroyed
Settlement is restricted	The forest is protected	Trees are replanted

LIVING TOGETHER

Almost half of the world's population now live in an **urban** environment, in towns or cities. About 32 million people live in Mexico City. More than 26 million people live in the Japanese cities of Tokyo and Yokohama, which have grown together to form one giant **conurbation**.

Urban sprawl As populations grow, cities spread outward, swallowing up the countryside and smaller settlements. The natural drainage system of the land is replaced as marshes are drained and streams are piped and converted to sewers and drains. Bulldozers level the soil, and cranes tower above the streets. Vast amounts of garbage are taken to city borders to be buried at landfill sites, or in less economically developed countries, garbage may just be dumped on the outskirts.

Changing faces The original town may now become the city center, consisting mostly of business and trade. The newer outer areas form **suburbs** which may include both factories and housing. Sometimes these outer areas become more popular than the old inner city, which is left to become run-down and neglected.

Urban renewal Renewing such districts is a constant challenge for town planners. Paris, the capital of France, has been transformed many times. In the 1850s, large areas of the unhealthy, old, medieval town were cleared and replaced with broad, well-drained, tree-lined avenues. In the 1960s and '70s, a second great rebuilding program took place. Run-down areas such as the Marais were restored, and the inner city markets of Les Halles were moved out.

Garbage operations in urban areas usually involve a huge system from collection to safe disposal, as shown here in Kyoto, Japan.

City needs Cities have many advantages. They can offer better services, better education, better healthcare, and more job opportunities. However, when so many people live in one place, they place a great strain on the natural environment. The growing population needs water and food. They need electricity, roads, and transportation. They produce garbage and human waste, which require **sanitation** systems.

The places in which people work, factories or offices, need even more resources than their homes. Industry accounts for 21 percent of all water usage worldwide.

Las Vegas may be a fantasy city, but the resources it needs to survive in a dry desert environment are very real.

Case study: Las Vegas, Nevada

Between 1900 and 2000, the population of Las Vegas, Nevada, grew from a few dozen to about 1.5 million. The city developed as a result of railroad links in the 1900s, the construction of the Hoover Dam in the 1930s, and the building of gambling casinos in the 1940s and '50s. It is a center of entertainment, and its hotels attract millions of visitors each year.

Desert city
Yet this city is built in a fragile desert environment. Rainfall is only about 4.4 inches (12 cm) a year. To supply the city with water and keep its golf courses green, the surrounding natural landscape had to be completely restructured. The Colorado River was dammed to create a vast mid-desert reservoir, Lake Mead. Water use still has to be limited and remains critical to the city's survival.

CONCRETE EVERYWHERE

In crowded towns and cities, the impact people have on the natural landscape is at its most extreme. Humans create a world of their own, a paved environment with cliffs of concrete, steel, brick, and glass. This extends deep underground, with drains, sewers, pipes, cables, and subways.

In some countries, particularly growing tourist areas such as Ibiza, Spain, construction is constantly underway.

Building space When there is little room to spread outward, buildings begin to rise higher. City-center skyscrapers or high-rise apartments offer large amounts of floor space within a small area of land. Their foundations are long tubes of steel called piers or piles, which are pushed into tough underground rock. In softer soils, a great raft of concrete reinforced with steel rods is built to support tall buildings.

Skyscrapers may make beautiful and prestigious buildings, but are not always suitable for housing. People like their own space, and children need to play outside. Housing to accommodate large numbers of people may include terraced homes or large estates.

City weather The city environment can even affect the weather. Heated buildings make cities warmer than the surrounding countryside, making snowfall less likely. High-rise buildings set up their own air currents, creating windy city centers.

Less impact The more harmful effects of a city on the environment can be reduced by careful planning. Rivers can be kept clean. Areas of natural landscape can be preserved within the city limits. Waste can be **recycled**.

Parks and gardens Green landscapes do survive within city parks and suburban gardens. Some are remnants of the natural landscape, but most are created to give people a chance to escape from the crowds, play sports, and relax. Many are also inhabited by wildlife. Cities provide an ideal habitat for many bird and mammal species.

Follow it through: city populations

Large numbers of people move to the city to find work

A lot of housing is needed

Nature's revenge

The city environment created by humans is just as destructible as the natural one. We forget this until it is torn apart by an earthquake or fire in a few minutes. Concrete breaks up and metals rust. If the city is abandoned to the rain and wind, plants soon root in the cracked pavements.

Chicago became one of the world's first high-rise cities when it was rebuilt after a fire in 1871. Chicago's concrete skyline rises high above Lake Michigan and the surrounding flat lands of the prairies.

Terraced homes and large estates are built

With too much housing, some areas begin to lack green space and become unattractive

Areas are renewed

Areas become run-down

TRANSPORTING PEOPLE

The more people there are, the more they need to be transported from one place to another. Within a city, people need to get to work. Emergency services need to get people to the hospital in a hurry. People need to travel abroad for vacations or business. Goods need to be transported, too.

Traffic needs transform the landscape and threaten the environment through construction and air pollution.

Human footprints

Moving around leaves its mark on the landscape. Even hikers can wear down a rocky mountain path. However, ships, trains, cars, and aircraft all leave a far bigger "footprint" on the land. These methods of transportation were developed to meet the needs of the population explosion. They also helped to make it happen.

Follow it through: car use

A growing population buys more cars ⟶ The roads become jammed ⟶ Bypasses and new roads are built

Population distribution Transportation plays a big part in **population distribution**. For example, many big towns developed around railroad junctions and seaports. Transportation encourages tourism and trade and opens up remote areas. All of these further transform the landscape.

Efficiency More roads mean more cars, and this leads to more roads being built. Is there any way out of this loop? One way is to limit access to the busiest roads or city centers, perhaps by charging drivers. Another is to greatly improve public transportation. Building a railroad track and building a road both affect the environment. However, a train can hold hundreds of people, while a car often holds only one. Trains are a more efficient method of transportation.

Take it further
Imagine you are building a new road. Think of the engineering problems you might face.

◆ Choose a route between two population centers.
◆ How might building your road affect the environment?
◆ How might it affect the way in which population is distributed?

Building roads in Xinjiang Province, China. With rapid expansion of China's economy, this has become a priority. There are more than 13.2 million vehicles in China that use the country's 825,000 miles (1.33 million km) of road.

Transportation solutions It is very difficult to build new transportation systems in densely populated city areas. New tracks for light railways or underground tunnels may require the demolition of existing housing. New city airports may cause noise and safety problems. One solution is an overhead **monorail**, as has been built in Sydney, Australia, but monorails rarely carry large numbers of passengers.

People buy more cars	Charges for road use and parking are increased	Public transportation is improved	Fewer roads need building
	Even more roads are built	Car use increases further	More jams and eventual gridlock

SUPPLYING THE WORLD

The population growth of the last hundred years has been marked by an ever-increasing demand for minerals, substances that need to be extracted from rock or soil. Before 1900, about 150 million barrels of oil were produced worldwide each year. By 2003, more than 78 million barrels were being produced every day.

An open-cast copper mine stretching into the distance in Chile.

Oil wells Oil, one of the most important minerals, is hard to get. A thick, black, sticky liquid, it is found underground, trapped in certain kinds of rock. It often lies beneath the seabed or in other fragile environments, including frozen Arctic tundra, tropical wetlands, and deserts. These environments are easily disturbed by drilling and production. Oil is processed to make gasoline and diesel for transportation, heating fuels, and numerous plastics and lubricants. The more people there are, the more oil is used.

Pits and shafts Think of all the metals used in a town as its population grows—cranes, trucks, cars, tools, coins, cans, and tins. All must be extracted from Earth. In quarries and open-cast mines, digging takes place at the surface, creating great pits and scars across

the landscape. In underground mines, shafts are either bored sideways into hillsides or downward, perhaps as much as 2.5 miles (4 km) into Earth. Rocks, ore, or coal may be blasted out with explosives, broken up with drills, or sliced with cutting machines. Some minerals may be flushed out with water or steam.

Mined landscapes When the minerals run out, the landscape may be left looking more like the surface of the Moon, surrounded by heaps of spoil. Shafts and pits fill with water and collapse, the land slips and slides. The site must be made safe, filled, and planted to return to a more stable state.

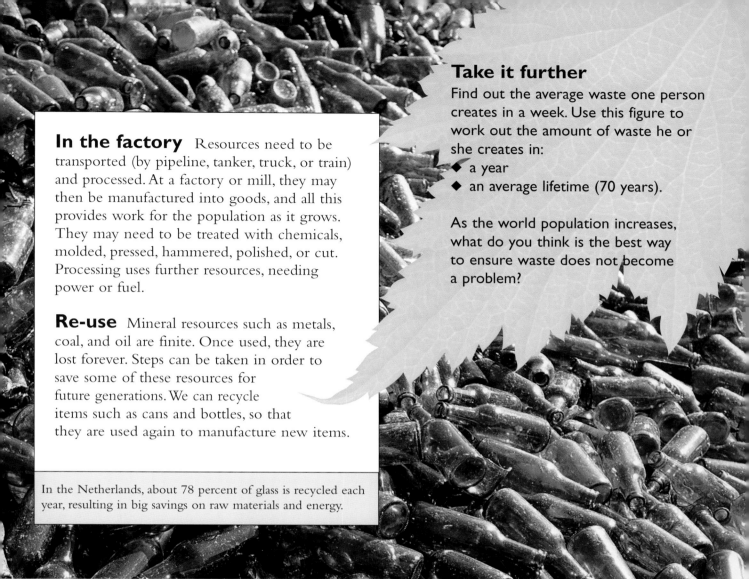

In the factory

Resources need to be transported (by pipeline, tanker, truck, or train) and processed. At a factory or mill, they may then be manufactured into goods, and all this provides work for the population as it grows. They may need to be treated with chemicals, molded, pressed, hammered, polished, or cut. Processing uses further resources, needing power or fuel.

Re-use

Mineral resources such as metals, coal, and oil are finite. Once used, they are lost forever. Steps can be taken in order to save some of these resources for future generations. We can recycle items such as cans and bottles, so that they are used again to manufacture new items.

In the Netherlands, about 78 percent of glass is recycled each year, resulting in big savings on raw materials and energy.

Take it further

Find out the average waste one person creates in a week. Use this figure to work out the amount of waste he or she creates in:

◆ a year
◆ an average lifetime (70 years).

As the world population increases, what do you think is the best way to ensure waste does not become a problem?

Case study: Nauru

Nauru is an island in the Pacific Ocean, with an area of just eight square miles (21 sq km). The islanders once believed it to be the only place in the world. However, after 1784, the island was discovered by outsiders—Germans, then British, Australians, and New Zealanders.

Phosphate mining

Beginning in 1888, the new settlers mined Nauru for phosphates—salts that are used to make fertilizers. These were exported in huge quantities for more than a century, as farming developed to feed the world population. However, mining made Nauru itself unfit for agriculture. The population of 9,000 had to crowd into the narrow coastal strip, while 90 percent of the island became a ghostly wasteland.

Nauru today

In 1993, the islanders were paid money for this lost land. Today, there are only a few years of mining left on the island. Plans are to restore the landscape, attract tourists with offshore diving, and to attract wealth by creating a tax haven.

ENERGY NEEDS

In the past 30 years, global demand for energy has almost doubled. In the next 20 years, it is set to soar by 60 percent. Large populations in industrial countries use huge amounts of electricity. This can be made or generated in many different ways. Nearly all of these methods have an impact on the landscape.

Burning up Electricity is generated by spinning **turbines**, which need to be powered. In 85 percent of power plants, this energy is provided by coal, oil, or natural gas. Their use has already changed the environment we live in through mining, drilling, and air pollution.

Nuclear power Nuclear fission releases a vast amount of energy. A reactor is used to turn this into a continuous supply of heat. Nuclear power requires extremely high standards of safety. A release of nuclear material may give out unseen **radioactivity**, which lingers in soil or water and endangers life.

Other major problems include the disposal of nuclear waste, whether underground or at sea. Such material may remain radioactive for hundreds or thousands of years.

Many industries consume fuel night and day, all year long.

Follow it through: geothermal energy

Rainwater seeps down through rocks and soil

Far beneath the surface, there are red hot volcanic rocks

Power from water Turbines can also be turned by flowing water to generate **hydroelectric power**. The water may come from a dammed river, lake, or waterfall, or from tidal currents in a river or sea. The building of a dam floods valleys. Interruption of flow affects not just the site of the dam but the whole course of the river and its basin. Tidal barrages across rivers also affect river flow, as well as plant growth and the migration of fish and birds.

Wind and sun Water is said to be a renewable energy source because it is not consumed in the generation process. Other "renewables" include power from the sun, which is used to activate panels of electric cells; geothermal energy, which uses volcanic heat from deep underground; and wind turbines. These giant windmills are often placed along ridges of hills or windy shores. They are mostly located in areas of low population, where people sometimes complain that they spoil the beauty of the natural landscape. For this reason, some countries plan to erect wind turbines out at sea.

Renewables do not cause pollution and are not dangerous. However, at the moment, they account for only 10 percent of the world's energy supply. It will be many years before they can produce cheap electricity on a truly industrial scale.

The solar furnace at Font Romeu, France, uses 9,600 mirrors to produce a heat of 5,400 °F (3,000 °C).

Save it! The U.S., with a population of 287.4 million, consumes more than 10 times as much energy as all of Africa, a continent with a population of 840 million. Africa uses less energy per head of population and recycles more. Many more economically developed countries waste energy and resources, for example, by driving gas-guzzling cars rather than ones with a low fuel consumption. Large savings can be made by cutting down on use and by insulating homes. That saves resources and conserves the land.

The water is heated, then wells back up to the surface or bursts through as steam

The steam turns turbines to generate power

No fuel is needed, so there is no pollution

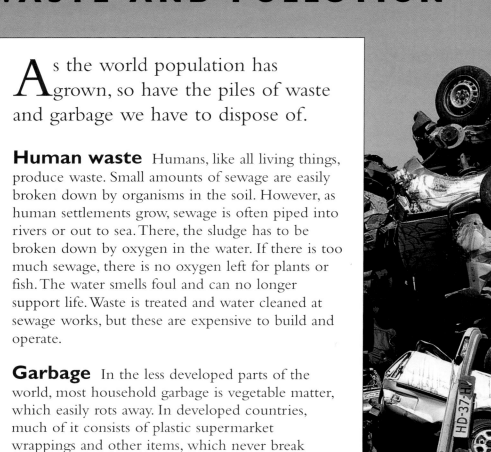

As the world population has grown, so have the piles of waste and garbage we have to dispose of.

Human waste Humans, like all living things, produce waste. Small amounts of sewage are easily broken down by organisms in the soil. However, as human settlements grow, sewage is often piped into rivers or out to sea. There, the sludge has to be broken down by oxygen in the water. If there is too much sewage, there is no oxygen left for plants or fish. The water smells foul and can no longer support life. Waste is treated and water cleaned at sewage works, but these are expensive to build and operate.

Garbage In the less developed parts of the world, most household garbage is vegetable matter, which easily rots away. In developed countries, much of it consists of plastic supermarket wrappings and other items, which never break down in the soil. Such waste can be reduced by recycling and by **biodegradable** packaging.

A graveyard for cars at Amsterdam, in the Netherlands.

Follow it through: pollution

Large numbers of people live in one place

There are high numbers of cars

Cars emit chemicals that become trapped by warm air over the city

The busy North Sea area.

Case study: The North Sea

The North Sea is a shallow arm of the Atlantic Ocean, lying between the United Kingdom, Belgium, the Netherlands, Germany, and Scandinavia. These are some of the most densely populated and industrialized lands in Europe. Oil is drilled in the seabed itself, there is fishing on a large scale, and some of the world's busiest shipping lanes. The North Sea is polluted by industrial metals, sewage, spoil from dredging, farmland run-offs, and shipping oil. Almost half of its pollution comes from rivers, such as the Rhine. The air and the rainfall is polluted by factories, oil refineries, power plants, and transportation. Countries bordering the sea are working to reduce pollution levels and conserve fisheries.

Population conflict

Household and industrial chemicals turn many garbage dumps and landfill sites into cocktails of toxic waste. This is land that becomes unsafe for future development. Refuse is often carried out of large population centers to areas where there are fewer people. Such dumps, however, are not pleasant neighbors. Rainwater may wash the poisons into soil and rivers. Fertilizers from farmland and waste from factories also poison land, rivers, and oceans. People in rural areas sometimes protest against disposal sites on their doorstep.

Poisoned air

Chemicals are released into the air by factories and by exhaust fumes from traffic and shipping. Gases given off by the burning of fossil fuels form clouds of smog over cities.

Climate change

Gases pumped into the atmosphere, the layer of air surrounding our planet, may be trapping in Earth's heat. Many scientists believe that this is causing the climate to warm very rapidly. Global warming could result in the melting of polar ice caps, the flooding of low-lying coasts, and desertification.

Sunlight reacts with chemicals, causing poor air quality

Increased incidence of health problems such as asthma
Plant and tree growth slows
Buildings and materials corrode faster than in rural areas

Car restrictions in urban areas may be introduced

EMIGRATION

People have always moved around the world. **Migration** can have a dramatic effect on population levels and distribution, as old lands are left behind (emigration) and new lands are settled (immigration). This, in turn, affects the way land is used.

Escaping poverty The most common reason for the movement of peoples is economic. People move to escape hunger or poverty. This may be because their population is too large to be supported by its resources, such as in Bangladesh, or because it is simply too poor to exploit those resources fully, such as in Ethiopia.

Case study: Lesotho's migrant workers

Lesotho is a small mountainous country surrounded on all sides by South Africa. It has a population of 2.2 million. Only 10.5 percent of the land is suitable for farming, so more than one-third of the adult male workforce leaves to work in the mines of South Africa. The money they send home to their families is the most important source of national income. Such division of the workforce affects agriculture, herding, settlement, and society.

When Lesotho men leave to work abroad, women stay behind to tend the crops.

Fleeing disaster

Sometimes it is the environment which affects migration, rather than the other way around. Erupting volcanoes, earthquakes, floods, or drought can force people to flee their homes. Some of these natural disasters can make the land uninhabitable. However, people often return once the disaster is over. People resettle the slopes of volcanoes despite the danger of another eruption, because volcanic soils are often very fertile.

Conflict

Persecution or conflict can set large numbers of people into motion when armies invade and people flee. World War II (1939–45) may have killed as many as 45 million people. It left the cities of Europe in ruins and made more than a million people into homeless **refugees**. Today, there are 22 million refugees worldwide. In Afghanistan, more than 23 years of war and drought have caused many people to flee the country, abandoning farms and bombed-out buildings.

Refugees on the road from Iran, returning to their home country of Afghanistan in 2002. Only seven percent of refugees go to developed countries. Most flee to neighboring developing countries, where resources are often limited.

Rice farming in Haiti is often hard, manual work.

Skill drain

Emigration can lead to a reduction of younger or skilled workers. In Haiti, the population growth remains relatively high at 1.7 percent a year, the highest rate in the Caribbean. However, many Haitians leave their homeland for Columbia, Venezuela, or the U.S., and this means that the country is losing its pool of young people. This leaves an aging population to work in the Haitian rice fields.

IMMIGRATION

Immigration can bring about as many changes as emigration. Immigrants boost populations—often with people who are eager to succeed. Migrants may bring new plants or farming methods, or new skills which help the economy and can therefore change the landscape.

Past migrations
Immigrants are usually attracted to countries where they believe they will find land and resources, or work. Native Americans populated the Americas thousands of years ago in search of new hunting grounds. Europeans arrived in the 1500s to found farming settlements. New migrants arrived from Europe in the 1800s to build cities and factories. Today, people of European origin live in Africa, Asia, Australia, and New Zealand, and people of African and Asian origin live in Europe, Australia, and the Americas.

Impact and change
Immigration has always had an impact on the host country. It was Dutch migrants to eastern England in the 1500s and 1600s who helped to drain the wetlands and develop the trade in woolen textiles. Sometimes migrants may bring about a reduction of population, by passing on new diseases, such as when the Spanish brought smallpox to Mexico in the 1500s.

In countries with stable population growth, immigration can increase the workforce and encourage economic development. However, one danger is that the incomers are exploited and paid low wages. They are forced to live in poor districts in poor housing.

Immigrant children outside a housing estate in Marseilles, France. As a Mediterranean port, Marseilles has always experienced high immigration. In the heart of the city, where many immigrants live, there is unhealthy housing, large blocks of apartments, and unemployment. No other place in France has such a high proportion of people living in poverty.

Wealthy immigrants Immigrants are not always poor. People from wealthy nations may move to more rural or "pleasant" areas, often for retirement. This tends to drive up property prices, making it more difficult for young local people to stay in the area. This can result in the depopulation of workers from farming or fishing villages. Large areas of rural France and Spain are settled by English, German, Dutch, and Scandinavian immigrants.

New influences Immigration brings cultural interaction and cosmopolitan influence. For many years, Australia restricted immigration on racial grounds, but today receives incomers from many Asian countries. Their contribution has transformed cities such as Sydney with new buildings and a variety of skills, from information technology to cooking. This has boosted tourism and attracted new businesses.

Take it further

Find out about immigration in your country. Look at government Web sites, census figures, or ask immigrant organizations.

◆ How many newcomers arrive in the country or neighborhood each year? What percentage is that of the whole population?
◆ What percentage of the population was born outside the country?
◆ Find out which ethnic minorities form significant groups.
◆ What jobs do immigrants do?
◆ Can you think of any ways immigration impacts the environment? For example, are migrant agricultural workers employed in your community?

A striking Hindu temple rises among traditionally English housing in Neasden, a suburb of London, UK.

A HEALTHIER WORLD

Health, population, and land are all closely linked. Poor harvests result in malnutrition and disease, and many young children die. Better healthcare means longer lives, reducing the economic need for poor people to have larger families.

An unhealthy swamp is cleared and drained in Malaysia.

Swamps and parasites Some of the world's worst illnesses are linked to the environment. Malaria is one of them, a fever caused by parasites. These are passed on to humans by the bite of certain mosquitoes, which breed in tropical swamps or stagnant water. There are about 300–500 million cases of malaria in the world each year, resulting in around a million deaths. Draining wetlands and ponds is part of the program for getting rid of this illness.

Diseases that affect cattle or other farm animals can be just as disastrous to farming communities as human ones.

Work-related illness Some illnesses which have a grave effect on population and the economy are caused by the work people do. For example, miners often breathe in dust from the coal or rock they drill, and this can damage their lungs, causing breathing difficulties or death.

Follow it through: disease in water

Lakes, ponds, and irrigation canals are used by villagers in tropical Africa

They become contaminated by sewage, causing snails in the water to carry a deadly parasite

Mass killers When deadly diseases reduce the population on a large scale, they affect farming, trade, and settlement, too. From 1347 to 1351, a plague called the Black Death probably killed about 75 million people in Europe and Asia. Villages and towns were abandoned.

Today, it is the disease HIV/AIDS which devastates towns, farming villages, and sometimes whole populations. In Zimbabwe, one-third of all people between 15 and 49 years of age suffer from this condition. This can leave farming areas neglected, which, in turn, makes it difficult for the people to support themselves.

Food aid saves lives . . . in the short term.

Village children are vaccinated in Goa, India.

World health Today, the World Health Organization coordinates the fight against disease on a global scale. Many of the worst illnesses can now be prevented, treated, or cured by drugs. However, these are expensive to buy and many less developed countries cannot afford them. Richer countries and charities often supply the poorer ones with medical **aid**.

The developed world also sends food aid to prevent malnutrition and starvation. This may prevent immediate loss of life, but, in the long run, projects that restore and conserve the land, to provide seed for hardy crops which will support a family in need, are also important.

| The parasite finds its way into humans | It causes a long-term illness called bilharziasis | The liver, kidneys, lungs, and gut may all be seriously damaged | Lakes and ponds have to be cleaned up |

A SUSTAINABLE PLANET

We cannot go back in time, to an age when the planet was green and there were no factories or crowded cities. Development is necessary to meet the needs of an increasing population. However, if we take away too many resources and destroy the environment, there will be little of value left for future generations. We need **sustainable development**.

A tree nursery in Mauritania, a very dry country which suffers from desertification. In 1988, the villagers set up a reforestation project. Since then, they have planted more than 40,000 saplings which have helped to slow the advancing desert.

Follow it through: using less

African villagers need fuel for cooking and warmth

They collect firewood, and as their numbers grow, they use more

Problem solving

One of the first demographers was Thomas Malthus (1766–1834). He believed that farming would not be able to provide enough food for the world's growing population, and that numbers would crash. In fact, science and technology helped humans avoid this disaster. Human intelligence will surely solve many such problems in the future.

Caring for the land

Sustainable development means moving forward carefully, in a way that can be supported over many generations. In this way, we can avoid a population crash or global disaster. This involves careful planning, wise management, and use of resources. Soil and farmland need conserving, and natural habitats such as forests, coasts, and oceans need protection. As far as possible, the resources that we use to develop our world should be renewable rather than finite.

Many countries now believe that industrial gases contribute to global warming and have agreed to cut emissions. At Kyoto, in Japan, in 1997, 38 industrial countries agreed to reduce emissions to 5.2 percent below 1990 levels between 2008 and 2012.

Take it further

Peat is taken from ancient bogs in Europe and sold as compost. However, sustainable creation of compost is possible:
1. Save uncooked vegetable leaves, tea leaves, potato peelings, etc. Do not save bread, meat, or cooked foods, which attract mice.
2. Place in a compost-making bin and allow to rot.
3. Eventually, the waste will form a crumbly, sweet-smelling mixture.
4. Dig it into soil in the autumn, ready for spring seedlings.

World resource distribution

Population levels and distribution are an important part of planning for sustainable development. Family planning programs and education help to reduce population growth. The fewer people there are, the less will be their impact on the planet. However, the distribution of resources across the world also needs to be considered. The world's more economically developed countries, mostly in the northern half of the world, use a higher share of resources. To change this situation is not an idealistic dream, but a necessity for our survival, a hard fact of life.

This cooker in India is solar-powered and needs no fuel.

Deforestation ▶ Without trees to hold soil together, the soil erodes ▶ One solution is to design a cheap but very efficient stove that uses much less wood

FUTURE WORLDS

What happens next? One estimate suggests a world population of 7.8 billion by the year 2025, and 9 billion by 2050. By 2200, it might be about 10 billion, and some say that at that point the population is unlikely to grow further.

How many?

Nobody can know for sure how the population will grow in the years to come. The United Nations is already down-scaling some of the larger estimates. How many humans can the planet support? Again, nobody knows. Some people believe we have already passed the red light. Others argue that as many as 44 billion could live on Earth.

Will we cope?

Further rises in population will have a major impact on the planet. This may mean an increase in the size of problems we are already facing. These include the loss of natural habitats such as forests, the spread of deserts, and the extinction of many animal species. We may see more wilderness lost to settlement or spoiled by mining and drilling and the spread of towns and cities. We may see global warming leading to climate change and flooding.

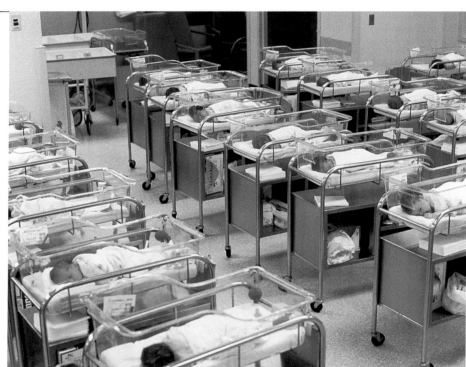

Newborn babies have the right to live in a healthy environment, with sufficient food and water. Can we provide this in the future?

Science challenge Some people believe there is little cause for alarm. Others disagree. Science and technology will clearly make a huge difference in medical research and immunization, and in farming methods.

Research into genes, unlocking the secrets of life, might affect our attitudes toward childbirth, families, and population, as well as toward the plants and animals with which we share the planet.

Life in space? One day, perhaps, humans may even be able to settle on other planets. By then, will we have learned how to look after our own?

A sustainable future Our understanding of life on Earth and the human environment has increased beyond all expectations in the last 100 years. In 2003, the United Nations reported that half of the world's population was now under 25 years of age. It is up to these people to make use of this knowledge, not for short-term gain, but for the benefit of future generations.

Plants have already been grown in laboratories in space. Scientific advances may help humans solve many of their problems.

Case study: The UN

The United Nations (UN), founded in 1945, has representatives from most of the governments in the world. It also runs many different agencies and organizations dealing with almost every aspect of society, from health to industry and the environment. Its successful work shows how important international cooperation is to the future.

The UN in Mongolia

Mongolia is the most sparsely populated country in Asia. It includes large areas of grassland and desert, and many of its people are nomadic herders. The UN, through its agencies, helps Mongolia in various ways:

◆ It provides equipment and training for census-taking.
◆ It has helped with the collection of data on population, the registration of households, and using this information in planning the country's development.
◆ It has hosted an international conference in Mongolia on sustainable development, which included studies of the traditional Mongolian diet.
◆ It helps train healthcare workers and fights disease.
◆ It provides information about family-planning.
◆ It has supported local and environmental conservation projects
◆ It has supported the development of industries.

GLOSSARY

Aid	Help, money, or food given by one country to help another.
Biodegradable	Made of substances that break down or rot naturally.
Birth control	Regulating the number of births by the deliberate prevention of childbirth.
Census	An official count of the population.
Contraception	Any method of preventing women from becoming pregnant, such as condoms or birth control pills.
Conurbation	Cities that have grown until they merge.
Demography	The scientific study of population and related subjects such as births, deaths, health, etc.
Domesticated	Animals tamed and bred by humans.
Ecosystem	The network of living things within a particular environment, and how they interact with each other.
Eco-tourism	The development of tourism that promotes concern for the environment rather than harming it.
Environment	The world around us.
Extinct	No longer surviving, having died out.
Fertilizer	A natural or chemical treatment designed to enrich the soil.
Genetic modification (GM)	The alteration of the genes which occur naturally within a species of plant or animal. The genes are the natural mechanism for passing on characteristics from one generation to another.
Global	Worldwide, affecting the whole planet.
Habitat	A type of natural environment as colonized by living things. Examples include grassland, hot desert, rainforest, or seashore.
Hydroelectric power	Energy produced by water-driven turbines.
Immunization	The protection someone is given against a particular disease; for example, by giving a person a very small dose of the same disease so that his or her body learns to resist it.
Intensive farming	Farming to produce the maximum amount of food possible for the lowest cost.
Migration	Movements of peoples from one region to another.
Monorail	A transportation system in which train cars are suspended from a single overhead rail.
Pesticide	A natural or chemical treatment designed to kill insects and other pests which harm crops.
Plantation	A large estate used for the commercial production of one particular crop.
Population	The number of people living within a given area.
Population density	The amount of population in relation to the area it occupies.
Population distribution	The way in which a population is spread out over the land.

Population explosion	A large and rapid rise in population.
Radioactivity	The disintegration of certain substances, such as uranium, that gives off dangerous rays.
Recycle	To make products using old or second-hand materials, in order to save natural resources.
Refugee	Someone who flees from one country to another as a result of war, famine, persecution, or poverty.
Sanitation	Drains, sewers, and waste disposal systems.
Suburb	The outlying districts surrounding a city or town.
Sustainable development	Developing a country in a way that can be maintained without exhausting its wealth or its resources.
Turbines	Machines driven by water or gases which generate electricity as they spin around.
Urban	To do with towns or cities.

FURTHER INFORMATION

Population Reference Bureau
A Web site that deals with demographic issues such as population, reproductive health, poverty, and the environment.

www.prb.org

Greenpeace
An organization devoted to the protection of the natural environment and biodiversity.

www.greenpeace.org

Friends of the Earth International
A campaigning organization with an environmental agenda opposing GM crops.

www.foei.org

Oxfam
This international campaigning organization deals with poverty, suffering, hunger, development, and trade. This site also contains a list of resources, activities, information, and ideas.

www.oxfam.org.

United Nations Division for Sustainable Development
The UN and its agencies play a global role in issues relating to population, environment, and development.

www.un.org/esa/sustdev

United States Census Bureau
Statistics on the U.S. 2000 census, along with links to resources on world population.

www.census.gov

INDEX